MW01058946

TIME TO BREAK
Free

MEDITATIONS FOR THE FIRST 100 DAYS
AFTER LEAVING AN ABUSIVE RELATIONSHIP

Judith R. Smith

INFORMATION & EDUCATIONAL SERVICES

Hazelden
Center City, Minnesota 55012-0176

1-800-328-0094
1-651-213-4590 (fax)
www.hazelden.org

Library of Congress Cataloging-in-Publication Data
Smith, Judith R.
     Time to break free : meditations for the first 100
days after leaving an abusive relationship / Judith R.
Smith.
          p.   cm.
     Includes bibliographical references.
     ISBN 1-56838-320-7
     1. Abused women—United States—Psychology.
2. Affirmations—United States. 3. Self-help tech-
niques—United States. I. Title.
HV6626.2.S55   1999
362.82'92—dc21   98-49897
                                          CIP

03 02 01 00 99   6 5 4 3 2 1

Cover design by David Spohn
Interior design by Nora Koch, Gravel Pit Publications
Typesetting by Nora Koch, Gravel Pit Publications

Dedication

By opening this book you have shown tremendous courage—you opened a door that can never be closed again. There now lies in your mind a spark of hope that maybe, just maybe, there is a way of a life other than one that has brought you confusion and pain. You have probably at some point said to yourself, *I want to live a better life.* Whether you begin reading this book today, decide to read it later, or seek another form of help, I promise you, there is a way your life can be different, there is a way your life can be better.

This book is dedicated to all of us who have survived, and most of all to those who didn't.

—Judith R. Smith

Acknowledgments

I offer my deepest and most sincere thanks to the following people: my children, Lacey and Max, my reasons—at the time—for breaking free, whose love gave me the courage to do so; my mother, Billie, without whose support and encouragement I would not have taken the steps to stay free; Arrow Moser, Henrietta LaVarta, JoAnne Hall, M.F.C.T., and Shari Biggs, M.F.C.C., the skilled professionals that provided me the education, support, and love necessary to break free; and Nicole Brown Simpson, whose violent and tragic death showed me the seriousness of domestic violence and its consequences.

Note to the Reader

Congratulations! You have just begun a journey that will help you gain control of your own life and break free from the pain you have felt in the past. I have written this book primarily to help women who are in the process of leaving an abusive or violent situation, but abuse can happen to anyone and can occur in any relationship. Parents, children, siblings, roommates, lovers, or family members—of either gender—are all capable of domestic violence. Women can be just as abusive as men, and domestic violence doesn't take place only between heterosexual couples. When I use the word *he* or *she* in this book, it's used as a general reference to keep the messages simple and concise. However you may be related to your abuser, or whatever gender that person is, please allow yourself the freedom to replace my words with your own as you continue your journey toward freedom from abuse.

As you will notice, I use the phrase *make a promise* quite often throughout the book. I am not suggesting that you are required to make promises to family members, friends, children, therapists, co-workers, or support groups. When I use the word *promise,* it is intended for you alone. A sincere promise to yourself is the most important promise you can ever make. In addition, I am not, by any means, saying that you must follow every suggestion in this book if you are to break free of domestic violence or abuse. My suggestions are intended to help you and increase the likelihood of your success. Don't worry if you miss a day. Don't skip ahead to catch up. Simply pick up the book and start where you left off.

This book is not intended to be used as your only source of support when you decide to break free. I strongly recommend that you seek additional help. You can choose a therapist, counselor, or support group. When choosing professional support, it is important that you find someone of your own gender that specializes in this field. A counselor without knowledge of domestic violence will not be able to understand or effectively assist you in your emotional healing. A support group dealing with a separate issue will not be able to offer the support you need to stay free. Most areas have a local YWCA or women's shelter that offers a support group for battered women, which will be invaluable to your healing. Again, prequalify your support team by making sure they are educated in the field of domestic violence and abuse.

It is with much empathy and respect that I offer this book to anyone wishing to break free from an abusive relationship. I truly hope that the words speak to you, and that in return, you hear them.

Congratulations on the courage you are showing by reading this book. May you be empowered in your healing, know in your heart that it's time to break free, and never again endure the pain you have felt in the past.

Day 1

Before I can begin my process of breaking free, I must admit to myself that I have been abused. Perhaps one person has abused me, or perhaps many. There may be reasons why this happened, but I don't have to think about the details and circumstances now. All I have to do today is admit to myself, "I have been abused."

Time to Break Free

Day 2

If my spouse or former spouse, the person I live with or used to live with, the parent of my child(ren), the person I am dating or have dated, or any person related to me has physically injured me or made me afraid of physical injury, I have experienced domestic violence. If I have been degraded, humiliated, controlled, threatened, or forced to do something I didn't want to do, I have been abused. For today, all I have to know is that I don't want to be abused anymore. I want it to stop, and I'm ready for it to stop. I will think of this as many times as I can for the next twenty-four hours.

Day 3

All I have to know today is that I'm willing to have my life be different. "Willingness" is the key to my freedom. When I'm open minded, when I'm ready to listen to ideas and suggestions, I'm already changing my life for the better.

If my abuser tries to get me back or wants to see me, he may promise all sorts of things. He may promise to attend Twelve Step meetings, go to counseling, cut down or quit drinking, cut down or quit using drugs, or never hurt me again. He may swear that he's sorry, say what he did was wrong, or blame it on something or someone else. He may act loving and apologetic, remorseful and emotional, or he may try to get me to feel sorry for him. His actions may turn angry, and he may threaten me, call me names, or yell at me. He may tell me I can't make it without him, no one will believe me, I'm crazy, or I'm being selfish. He may say many things to me, but one thing I can count on: He will say anything he can think of to get what he wants. I need to know that all of these claims are typical of abusers. He may use different words, but the fact that he says them is typical of any abuser. The best thing I can do is not put myself in the position of having to listen to any of it. I do not have to listen to his excuses or promises anymore. And for today, I won't.

Day 5

Today I will make a promise to have no contact with my abuser. I need this time to heal, and I can't do it the right way if I'm still seeing, talking to, or spending time with my abuser. Even if I don't understand this way of thinking, I promise to try it. Often, when we're in the middle of a situation, we need to step back in order to see it clearly. The most important thing for me to do during this difficult time is to refrain from having any contact with my abuser, to step back so I can see clearly.

Time to Break Free

Day 6

Today I will begin keeping a journal of all my thoughts and feelings. I may resist doing this at first, but I will make a commitment to writing at least one thought at the end of each day. By putting my thoughts down on paper, I see things more clearly. I can also go back and read them at a later date, to see how I have been able to change over time. Even if I have to force myself to write one sentence each day, I will do so. I know it's for my own good, and I can use all the "good" I can get.

Day 7

While being abused I learned to ignore or not notice those things that were painful. Today I will start practicing "focus." Taking care of my own or my children's needs, whatever they may be, requires my total attention. When I have a hard time staying focused on important things, I can practice by paying attention to little things. When I'm involved in a task, I will pay total attention to what I'm doing at the time, whether it be cooking, sewing, watching a television show, raking leaves, gardening, reading, cleaning house, or doing laundry. I can learn to be aware of my actions, my surroundings, and my task plan, and I can perform each task to the best of my ability. I will try not to let my mind wander with negative thoughts about myself or my life. I may have to keep pulling my thoughts back, time and time again, but it will get easier.

Time to Break Free

Day 8

Today I will do one thing more than I think I can do. If I'm too tired or depressed to get out of bed, I will not only get up but also take a shower. If I don't have the energy to go to work, I will get dressed and drive to the parking lot of my job. If I just can't face the world, I will walk to the end of the street and back. I will reach a little further than whatever I believe my limitations to be. Usually, when I take that little extra step, it seems easier than I thought it would, and I feel better too.

Day 9

I do not have to feel ashamed if I choose to stay with a friend or move into a shelter for battered women. I do not have to make excuses for my abuser anymore. I do not have to hide or lie about the bruises and wounds. I do not have to pretend that nothing is wrong, because something is wrong—very wrong. I have been treated badly, terribly, and illegally. It is not my fault and I have done nothing to deserve being abused. Today I will know in my heart that I am doing the best I can to take care of myself and, if I have children, that I am taking care of all of us. I will keep reminding myself that I'm doing the best I can to keep myself and my children safe.

Time to Break Free

Day 10

If I'm still involved in some way with my abuser, it's important for me to have a safety plan. The plan may be to have an emergency bag packed, in case I have to leave quickly. It should contain money, keys, clothing, important phone numbers, and whatever else I may need. My plan may be to have an extra set of car keys hidden somewhere or to have a secret bank account. I may also need to talk to my children about my plan. Hopefully my plan will be more than just a safe-deposit box for my family to find in the event of my death. Domestic violence is serious, and I will take protecting myself seriously.

Day 11

There will be days when my mind is full of painful thoughts. I may be remembering all the details of abusive incidents. I may be thinking about every word that was said, how I could have acted differently, or how I could have prevented what happened. These are not good thoughts for me to have because they can hurt me more than help me. Today I will imagine that these thoughts are in a giant bank vault and that I can close the heavy door on them. They will still be there to look at later, but I don't have to think of them today. I will choose to wait until I'm stronger. It may be hard to close the door at first, but I will begin to practice doing it today.

Time to Break Free

Day 12

It's not okay to be hit. I do not like being hit, and I don't want it to happen again. Today I will realize that there's help for me and that I don't have to be ashamed of being hurt by someone. Domestic violence is against the law. I do not have to feel embarrassed about what someone else has done to me. Making the choice to get help takes courage, and I will find that courage within myself.

Day 13

Today I will remember that there are many women who are going through the same experience as I am, and I'm not alone. I can reach out to others when I'm ready; I will find other women who will understand. I can attend a support group, call a hot line, or keep telling myself, "I'm not alone. I'm not alone." Just knowing this makes me feel better. But if I break the silence and tell someone I trust, I feel even better.

I am willing to ask for help, even if I feel embarrassed, ashamed, or guilty. In spite of what I'm feeling, I can ask for help. I do not have to ask my abuser or any of his friends for help. There are many other places I can go, and today I will find out what my options are. One of the hardest things to let go of is how ashamed I feel. I might feel that the abuse was my fault because I didn't leave earlier, or that people might think I stayed because being hurt was okay with me. I might feel guilty for exposing my children to such a terrible situation, or that I did not protect them the way I "should" have. Feeling such shame can stop many women from seeking the help they need, but not me. All I have to do today is be willing to ask for help from someone I trust. This is a big step in my life, and I'm proud of my decision and the strength I have found. I do not have to go by myself through the pain of being abused. I will ask for help because I do not have to be alone anymore.

Day 15

In these first days after leaving my abuser, I am very vulnerable, and I need to remember that decisions I make during this time may not be in the best interest of me or my children. Today I promise myself that I will listen to other people who know about domestic violence. I will listen to what they have to say, their suggestions, and their ideas. I may not agree with them now, but I will still listen. Whether I seek out a counselor, a therapist, a group facilitator, or a combination of these, I will listen to their experiences and honor their knowledge. My situation is much like those of all the people they have helped before I came along.

Time to Break Free

Day 16

Some days, every aspect of my life seems over-whelming and crazy, and I feel so confused. On these days, I need to remember that I only have to do what needs to be done today. I do not have to worry about next week, next month, or next year—only what needs to be done today. I can make a list of things to do. When I finish some-thing on my list, I can cross it off and feel proud of what I've accomplished, even if it's as simple as doing the dishes or making a phone call. When I accomplish something, I can be proud of myself.

Day 17

Unless I or my children are in immediate danger, I do not have to make spur-of-the-moment decisions. I don't have to decide today what I'm going to do with the rest of my life. I can take time to look at my options and then make informed choices. I can seek the advice of a trusted friend or acquaintance, read appropriate materials, call agencies that might be of assistance, or simply take the time to think about what I really want. Where do I want to live? What kind of job would I like to have? I may feel more comfortable deciding on a simple thing, like what to make for dinner tonight. I don't have to feel rushed in my plans or decisions. I can take my time, and that's exactly what it is: *my* time.

I do not have to share everything I'm feeling with my children. Children in domestic violence situations often take on the role of a parent, believing it's their job to protect and take care of their mother or father. I will not put my children in that position. I am the parent, and they are the children. They might have been feeling responsible for me for a long time, and it may be hard for us to "relearn" how to act with each other. Today I will begin trying. Children should be able to enjoy being children, and today I promise to give them that gift.

Day 19

If I'm feeling lost and confused, I will remind myself that going back to my abuser is not going to change the way I feel. Going back is just that—going backward. Today I choose to go forward, and I make a promise to myself to take each day as it comes. Going back is not an option.

My abuser may have had a hard life. The stories of his childhood may be sad, and I wish I could help him. But I have tried to help him for a long time now. It didn't work. Today it's time to start helping me. Saying good-bye to helping him and saying hello to helping me does not make me a selfish person. It makes me a capable, courageous, intelligent person, despite what anyone else thinks or says. I did not cause his problems, and I can't save him from them. The person I choose to help is me. The life I choose to save is my own.

Day 21

When others tell me that my being hurt "wasn't that bad," they are wrong. When they tell me I'm "too sensitive" or "making a big deal out of nothing," they are wrong. When most people do something wrong, they take responsibility for their actions. Abusers want to blame others, believe there is a good reason for what they've done, or make it seem less important than it really is. Spousal abuse is when any person physically injures—whether it's minor or serious—their spouse or any person they are living with, used to live with, or the parent of their child. Spousal abuse is a felony, and it is not okay with me.

Time to Break Free

Day 22

Sometimes I may think that my experience is different from anyone else's or that no one knows my abuser the way I do. It is during these times that I remind myself I'm not the only person this has happened to. I am willing to admit that there are other women who know more about this than I do, and I can ask their opinion of what I'm thinking or planning. In my first weeks of healing, I may have listened to the stories or advice of other abused people. I may have thought that my abuser was different, but I must understand that he's not. I will pay attention to the similarities of abusers instead of the differences between them, and I will open up to asking the opinions of people who have been able to break free.

Day 23

A restraining order is a legal document issued by a court that says my abuser cannot see me, talk to me, bother me, call me, threaten me, or hurt me. The thought of getting a restraining order can be scary. I may be terrified of what my abuser will do if I get one. But a restraining order can protect me from my abuser and from my own indecision. I can't let my abuser come over one day and not the next. I must respect the restraining order just as I want my abuser to. If I do decide to get one, I will have to fill out papers and have a judge sign them. Some counties have restraining order "clinics" and volunteers to help with the paperwork. Today I will call a women's center or shelter and find out how to get a restraining order in my county so I can get one now or in the future. If I've already decided to get one, I will take a good friend, or someone from an agency that helps women, with me for support. I will not wait until the last minute to find out how this process works.

Time to Break Free

Day 24

Today I realize I don't have to answer the phone. I can let it ring, unplug it, take it off the hook, get an answering machine, or change my phone number. Even if I feel confused about my abuser and might even miss hearing his voice or talking to him, I do not have to talk to him or to anyone I don't want to talk to. Deciding what I want is new for me, and this includes discovering who I like talking to and who I don't. While I'm healing, it's better not to talk to my abuser or to people who don't emotionally support me. I have the right to talk to people whom I like, people that treat me the way I really want to be treated.

Day 25

In order to make someone else happy or convince myself that someday my life would, as if by magic, get better, I have put my life on hold. I know now that it didn't work. The magic day never came, and I was waiting and hoping for happiness that was never going to come. I am worthy of being happy, of having people love me the way I want to be loved, and of making my own choices about what happens to me. It's my life. Today I take it back.

Time to Break Free

Day 26

I don't always get to know why things happen. I may spend hours, even days, trying to figure out why bad things have happened to me. I may get caught up in trying to understand other people, situations, and even my own thoughts. Today I will accept that I don't have to know why things are the way they are. Instead I can pay attention to healing, growing, and learning.

Day 27

"Acceptance" does not mean that I have to like what has happened to me or that it was okay with me, nor does it mean forgetting or forgiving. It means I accept the fact that it is happening or has happened. I accept the fact that some people hurt others, but I don't have to like it, and I don't have to be a part of it. Today I will accept the fact that I have been hurt, and I accept the fact that I didn't like it.

Time to Break Free

Day 28

Each day I feel stronger and stronger. I am learning how to make decisions that feel right. I can decide for myself what outfit to wear, what to cook for dinner, what movie to watch, or where I will go on vacation. I can do things on my own that I didn't know I could do. I will take a moment now to think of my accomplishments, even of the simplest tasks. I might even write them down so I can read them later.

Day 29

Domestic violence is more than physical abuse. I used to think that, if I didn't have a black eye or bruises, I wasn't in an abusive relationship. But abuse comes in different forms. It is not okay to hit, push, shove, kick, punch, stab, shoot, cut, rape, throw things at, or bruise your partner. It's also not okay to name call, belittle, threaten, degrade, humiliate, brainwash, coerce, or criticize your partner. Even though the items on the second list do not include acts of physical violence, they are still considered abusive. Today I will realize that any person who has lived with abuse, whether it was physical, verbal, or emotional, has been through a war zone. I can have compassion for all of them, including myself.

Time to Break Free

Day 30

Today I celebrate thirty days of taking care of myself. I plan to do something special for myself, something that I will truly enjoy, something nurturing. While my life still has ups and downs, there are fewer downs than there used to be. I know I have a ways to go, but I'm grateful for coming this far and for finding self-acceptance and courage in a surprising place—inside of myself.

Day 31

Today I will try to understand that abuse is not my fault, and that it's not me that's crazy when others treat me badly. Even when they tell me it's my fault or I'm crazy, I will keep telling myself it's not true. I will keep telling myself I'm not at fault, again and again, until I believe it. I can believe it because it's the truth. The hurt others have caused me is not my fault. I'm not crazy.

Time to Break Free

Day 32

Because of all I have gone and am going through, there may be times when I feel like I have little or no energy. During these times, I will be gentle with myself. I have been through a lot. I need time to recover. I will remember that having an abuser removed is major surgery of the soul. I need time to heal, and I need rest. It is okay for me to let myself take it easy.

Day 33

I will hug my children at least two times a day, no matter what. Even when my children are being disruptive and disobedient, I will keep reminding myself that they are in need of my attention and might not know how to ask for it. To the best of my ability, I will show my children I love them by talking to them, listening to them, and being emotionally available to them. I believe that we will get through this—together.

Time to Break Free

Day 34

Although he may ask, and although I may be tempted to, I do not have to tell my abuser what is happening in my life. I do not have to tell him where I am, what I'm doing, or how I'm feeling. I don't even have to talk to my abuser at all. I can take time to think about my choices and talk to other women who understand what I'm going through. I do not have to share anything about myself with someone who has a history of abusing others.

Day 35

Sometimes I feel so guilty that the pain is almost more than I can bear. I might be thinking of how I've exposed myself and my children to the nightmare of violence and abuse. I might be thinking of how I stayed too long before I left. What I have to learn and become comfortable with is the fact that I did the best I could under the circumstances. I was caught in a trap and didn't know how to get out. That was then, and this is now. Today is different, and I can now make better choices. I will keep telling myself that I did the best I could. I did the best I could. I did the best I could.

Time to Break Free

Day 36

Some days my life feels so confusing and over-whelming that I think I'll scream. Sometimes life is like moving from one place to another. When I move into a new house, it is unorganized and chaotic until everything gets put in the right place. In life, my emotions and thoughts are often like the new house full of boxes. I am learning how to unpack one emotional "box" at a time, throw out what I no longer need, and put what I do need in its proper place. It's a hard job, but it's all part of the process of taking back my life. When my emotional work gets too hectic, I will remember to keep things simple, to deal with one "box" at a time. Eventually, I'll get through the craziness, and everything will be in its rightful place.

Day 37

In matters of divorce that involve child custody and visitation rights, there might be times when I have no choice but to see my abuser, talk while he's in the room, or talk directly to him. During these times, I will ask someone I trust to go with me to the appointment. There are agencies that have volunteers available for situations like mine. I don't have to see my abuser alone, and I don't have to talk to him alone. Many agencies or legal officials will hold separate custody or investigation interviews if I request one. All I have to do is call and make the request by explaining that this is a domestic violence situation. I will plan ahead when I know I will have to see my abuser and not wait until the last minute to ask for help.

Time to Break Free

Day 38

People may have said about my abuser, "But he's such a nice guy." It's probably true because one thing that most batterers have in common is the ability to be charming. Many batterers are attentive, sensitive, exciting, and affectionate to their partners when they're not battering them. Batterers can also be of any age, any race, any religion, or any occupation. They may have high or low intelligence, be social or antisocial, and often appear kind and loving to those who aren't living with them. Others may think I've been in love with the abuse, but that's not true. I was in love, or may still be in love, with the charming side of my abuser, and it was one of the biggest reasons I stayed. But now I know the truth. All parts of my abuser come in the same package. I can't have the good without the bad. I want a better life now, and I'm going to have it.

Day 39

Today I promise myself to stay free. Even if I take one or ten steps backward, I will continue with what I've learned. If I call, engage in intimate conversation, or make plans with my abuser, I realize these are choices that are not good for me. If I find myself fantasizing about my abuser, I will bring myself back to the reality of my situation. If I'm unhappy with the progress of my healing, or I can't see any positive results, I trust that someday I will. Like a mountain climber, if I just keep climbing up, eventually I will get to the top.

"Boundaries" are limits I set in my life to let others know what is okay and not okay with me. I probably haven't had any boundaries for a long time, or if I did, I changed them to make other people happy. One of my boundaries is that it's not okay for anyone to hit me. Another boundary is that it's not okay for anyone to call me names or belittle me. These boundaries might have been violated, and I might not have done anything about it. Because I have been abused and my boundaries were ignored for so long, what I will allow and won't allow in my life has become vague and clouded. I will practice setting simple boundaries with myself first. "I don't want to watch this television show" or, "I don't want to eat at that restaurant" are good places to start. If I learn to acknowledge and tell myself what I want, telling other people will get easier.

Day 41

One of the most common questions people ask me is, "Why didn't you leave?" There are many reasons why people stay in abusive relationships, but I don't have to explain them to people who don't understand domestic violence. I may choose to say, "I don't really know, but I'm working on it with my counselor" or, "It's really very personal, and I'd rather not talk about it." I don't have to feel ashamed of what other people don't understand. No one can make me feel embarrassed about my life because of how "they" see it. What's important is how I see it and what I'm doing about it.

Time to Break Free

Day 42

There may be times when I still feel sorry for my abuser. He may remind me of the things that happened in his life that hurt him, or he may blame others in his life for his abusive behavior. He may cry or feel sorry for what he's done. He may beg my forgiveness and ask me to come back. But today I realize that, even though someone or something hurt him, he does not have the right to hurt me or my children.

Day 43

My family may be difficult to handle after I've left my abuser, especially if they never knew our relationship was abusive. My family, with all their good intentions, may tell me what to do, ask questions, or become critical of my past. They may behave this way because they are abusive too, or perhaps they just don't understand. It's confusing at times, especially when I need my family's support or financial help. I'm not emotionally strong enough to listen to their negative comments. This is the perfect time to find a support group or begin counseling, so I can begin to share my feelings and heal in a safe place. My family may love me in their own way, but I need to be able to talk to people that don't want anything from me. Getting outside help doesn't mean I don't love or need my family; it means I'm doing all I can to help myself.

Time to Break Free

Day 44

No one has the right to tell me who my friends can be, where I can go, or what I can do. I have the right to make decisions for myself. I am not the property of anyone. Today I will start thinking about things I would like to do, places I would like to go, and people I would like to see. I might not even know what these things will be—I may never have thought I could dream of such things—but today I will start thinking about them.

Day 45

There is a "Higher Power" that is greater and stronger than I am. It may be God or any spiritual figure or belief. I do not necessarily have to go to church or be a religious person to believe in a Higher Power. All I have to know is that this Higher Power is available to help me. This may be hard to believe because of all the hurtful things that have happened to me. I may feel that I've been ignored, betrayed, or punished for something I did wrong. But I realize these are normal feelings for anyone who has been through a trauma. I feel better knowing that my feelings are normal, but I feel even better knowing I am willing to believe in this Higher Power that loves me.

Time to Break Free

Day 46

Today I will believe my children. When they express their feelings, I will believe them and won't try to minimize their feelings. If they tell me they're afraid, I'll believe them. If they want a light on during the night, I'll allow it. If they have a nightmare, I'll comfort them. If they don't want to go to certain places that feel scary, I'll respect their wishes. I will also respect my own feelings, and I won't try to minimize them. If I want to sleep with the light on, I will. If I feel like crying, I'll cry. We all may be suffering from post-traumatic stress syndrome, a condition that occurs after a severe trauma or after a long period of unbearable circumstances. If I want to learn more about this syndrome, I will. When my children trust me enough to share their feelings, I will value their trust by listening. Listening doesn't mean I have to fix their problems; it means simply being there emotionally for my children. Today I promise to listen to my children and believe their feelings to be true, because they are.

Day 47

There may be times when I consider going back to my abuser. It may be because of money, shelter, the kids, loneliness, sex, or jealousy. Maybe I want to help him, maybe I'm believing his promises. Before I consider "trying again," I will commit to having no contact with my abuser for two weeks. No letters, no phone calls, no visits. During these two weeks I promise to attend a support group for abused women or begin counseling with a woman who is experienced in the area of domestic violence. Two weeks to make a major decision isn't very long, and I will, at the very least, take this time for myself and my children. If my abuser is pressuring me to hurry and move back in, I will tell him that I need two weeks without talking to him in order to decide. I do not promise that in two weeks I'll come back—I promise that in two weeks I will make my decision.

Time to Break Free

Day 48

Today I will make a list of things I like about myself. I will write about my good qualities and the things I feel I do well. I'll put a date on the list so that in the future, when I read it, I will remember how I'm feeling now. I'll make a new list every thirty days because, even if it seems silly, I realize that this is part of learning how to like and appreciate myself.

Day 49

I have become quite good at blocking out what I don't want to hear or notice. Right in the middle of hearing someone scream, or during a crisis, I can zone out and not hear or see a thing. I have become such an expert at this that, even when not in crisis, I don't hear what other people are saying, including my children. I can be looking straight ahead at the television and not know what I'm watching. This is a survival skill that I acquired in order to protect myself from frightening or potentially dangerous situations. It has served me well in the past, but it no longer serves me. It is difficult to change this pattern, but now that I'm aware of my "zoning out" behavior, I can learn to consciously come back to the real world. Today I will practice paying attention and tuning in to the sounds and events around me.

Time to Break Free

Day 50

When I realize that I don't want to be controlled anymore, I become more aware of friends or family members trying to control me. I may even become overly sensitive to their advice or opinions and feel like they're trying to tell me what to do. When this happens I can say, "Thank you for your opinion, but I'm trying to make my own decisions, and I need you to help me learn how." Hopefully, they will hear me and care for me enough to respect my request. If not, I can let them share their opinions, knowing that I don't have to live by their suggestions. If this is too difficult for me, perhaps I can spend less time with these people. Today I will begin to take control of my own life and my own decisions.

Day 51

When I was with my abuser, I didn't know how common my situation was. I didn't know that I was caught in the "cycle of violence." For the next three days, I will learn all I can about this cycle and try to understand how it occurred in my life. The cycle begins with the tension-building phase. During this phase, I may have a feeling that something is going to happen, or I may notice certain behavior in my abuser. He may be in a bad mood, act more jealous than usual, slam doors or want to be alone, be short or sarcastic in his comments, give me dirty looks, or do something else that sends a message that something is wrong. I may try to comfort him, calm him, or find out what the problem is. I, or the children, may "walk on eggshells" so as not to aggravate him further or cause any additional problems. We may avoid him or act especially nice, trying to initiate positive conversation as our tension and fear build. This phase can last for a few minutes, or it can go on for days. Today I will recall the times when this phase occurred in my life. I will write about what my abuser did or said, and how I felt when it was happening.

The second phase of the cycle of violence is known as the acute battering incident. In this phase the actual abuse occurs. The incident can involve abuse as minimal as accusing, name calling, or shouting. The incident can also involve abuse as damaging as intense verbal abuse, slapping, pushing, or throwing objects. In some cases the incident can be as extreme as punching, kicking, raping, or using a weapon. To say the least, this phase can cause severe emotional damage as well as temporary or permanent physical damage, and even death. The incident can happen in a few minutes, but often it lasts anywhere from two to twenty-four hours. Today I will write about the times this phase occurred in my life. I will write about what my abuser did or said, and how I felt when it was happening. If this is too difficult for me to do alone, I can choose to work with a therapist or counselor. I do not have to do this all in one day, and I can take as much time as I need to heal. There are no right or wrong answers, nor can I work through my healing process too quickly or too slowly. I will heal at the pace that feels right for me. When my list is complete, I can keep it and put it away. In the days to come, if I forget the truth about what happened to me, I can remind myself by taking it out and reading it.

The third phase of the cycle of violence is known as the honeymoon phase. In this phase, the incident has ended, and there seems to be a calm after the storm. It can simply be the absence of yelling or hitting, or it can include apologies from the abuser as well as tears, remorse, gifts, promises, and sex. This is usually the time in which the battered woman tries to bargain with the abuser. If he is remorseful, she will usually ask for something she wants. She may ask him to stop drinking, stop using drugs, go to counseling, or never abuse her again. The abuser may agree at this point, as he may feel that if he doesn't, she'll leave. The honeymoon phase is one of the biggest reasons why abused women don't leave. They cling to the hope that the relationship will get better, holding tight to the fantasy of a loving relationship as she pictures it in her mind. These women wish desperately to believe their abuser's promises, and most of the time they do, until the next incident occurs. The sad part is that, as the abusive relationship continues, this phase becomes shorter, less pleasurable, and eventually may become nonexistent. When the abused woman continues to believe and stay with the abuser, he believes the chances of her leaving to be less. The abuse then becomes increasingly violent, and the incidents increase in severity. Today I will write or talk about the times this phase occurred in my life. I will remember what my abuser did or said, and how I felt when it was happening. I will write about the promises that were made to me, which ones were kept, and which ones were not.

Time to Break Free

Day 54

Today I will accept my circumstances, even if I don't know what's going to happen next or where I'm going from here. I accept the fact that I'm an abused woman, that I've left an abusive person, and that I might not have a clue as to why this has happened to me. I accept the fact that I may not know what to do next. I may not have all the answers, but I know that I refuse to be abused any longer. I know I'm going in the right direction, and for now, that's all that matters.

Day 55

Today I'll make a list of things that I would like to do, just for me and no one else. My list can contain things I've always wanted to do: things that are fun, things that are relaxing, or things I've only dreamed of doing. I am beginning to realize what I want instead of what someone else tells me to want. I'm also beginning to realize that the things I dream of doing can be achieved.

I've learned a lot about domestic violence since I've left my abuser, and I feel excited about my newly found knowledge. I may find myself wanting to help other abused people by sharing my own story. It is very important that, before I do this, I first commit to my own healing. I must work through my own issues of abuse and get to a place of stability, contentment, and peace. When I have accomplished this, if I still have the desire to help other people, I can become involved with agencies or organizations that need my help. I can be a very important asset to other abused people when I do my own work first.

Day 57

Today I will begin to learn how to love myself. I will begin by simply looking in the mirror and saying out loud, "I am lovable." It may sound silly and feel even sillier, but only because I don't believe it's true. I will practice doing this at least once every day. The more I practice, the more comfortable it will feel. Eventually, I will believe it to be true. I *am* lovable.

Time to Break Free

Day 58

There are days when I feel impatient with the way my life is going. Maybe my emotional healing isn't happening fast enough for me, and I feel angry or frustrated. Maybe I'm having financial problems, or my job doesn't satisfy me. Maybe caring for my children is tiring, or I can't find time for myself. Today I will practice being patient. Sometimes the hardest thing to do is to do nothing—to wait for events to unfold in their own time. I can learn to relax and stop trying to force things to happen. I can't control everything in my life, and today I will stop trying. I don't have to achieve all my goals in one day or even one month. As hard as it may seem, for today, I will be a patient person.

Day 59

Sometimes I don't feel that I'm getting enough information or personal help from my support group, friends, or family. At times like these, I realize that I might need help from a professional counselor or therapist. Today I will find the courage to make a consultation appointment with a female therapist, and I will also remember that the purpose of a consultation is to see whether we can work together. One of the most important questions I will ask a therapist is whether she has experience in the area of domestic violence. If I don't like the first therapist I meet with, I can meet with others until I find one with whom I feel comfortable and safe.

Time to Break Free

Day 60

Today I celebrate sixty days of my freedom. It feels so good, yet scary at the same time. The thought of being on my own was always so frightening, but I'm beginning to believe I can do it. My worst day now is better than my best day when I was being abused. If I can make it for sixty days, I know I can make it for more.

Day 61

As much as I may love my children, I cannot provide them with the same help as a counselor or support group of their peers can. My children have different needs for their emotional healing than I have for mine. Perhaps they would feel more comfortable talking to a therapist or support group than they would talking to me. Perhaps they have feelings about me that they won't tell me, but that they would share with a professional. Today I will make time to look into finding help for my children. I will respect their need for privacy in their own healing. Being a good parent is also being willing to let someone else help me with my children.

Today I will practice looking at situations and learning the difference between "taking action" and "letting go." Many times I need to take care of things that seem difficult or overwhelming, and I have to push myself to get them done because I know they are necessary or good for me. This is called taking action. There are other times when I want things to get done a certain way or in a certain amount of time. These things may not be within my control, and I may feel frustrated that I can't change them when or how I want to. This is when it's important to learn the art of letting go, which is usually harder than taking action. I will practice taking action when I need to and letting go of the things I have no control over.

Day 63

In the United States, over half of the entire female population will experience physical abuse at least once in their lifetime. Of those women, approximately one-third will be battered regularly. Domestic violence pays no attention to income, race, religion, education, age, sexual orientation, or lifestyle. If I feel I'm different from other abused women, I must remember that we all experience the same feelings and share a common desire—we don't want to be hurt anymore.

Time to Break Free

Day 64

Today I accept the fact that I have made mistakes. I find comfort in knowing that, in the past, I did what I thought was right at the time. What makes my mistakes seem so bad is that I judge them by what I know today. I know more than I did then, and less than I will tomorrow. I trust that, in the future, I will not make the same mistakes. I have more information now, and I will be able to handle things differently and make wiser choices. I accept myself for who I was then and for who I am today.

Day 65

I need not feel guilty when I have good feelings or when I feel happy. I may be so used to feeling bad that when I feel good about myself, it feels awkward and strange. Feeling good is okay, and feeling different is okay. When I begin to live without terror or crisis, it may be difficult at first, but after a while, "different" becomes familiar. I've lived in pain for a long time now, and it's okay for me to like feeling good.

Time to Break Free

Day 66

Balance is an important thing to have in my life. I need to have a balance between work (any difficult task) and play. I need to know when it's time to stop working and enjoy myself, or when it's time to stop having fun and get down to business. As I learn balance, I may want to make a schedule for myself to see how I spend my time. Helpful tools like this will guide me toward achieving balance in my life.

Day 67

Being alone has its benefits, but I also need to be aware of when it's time to be with or make new friends. I might be afraid to have a social life because of the betrayal I have experienced in the past. It's okay for me to want to be alone and enjoy being alone, but making new female friends is important too. I can choose safe places to make friends, like a support group, Twelve Step meeting, church, or class. I can also make new friends without telling them all the details of my life. Today I will ask one woman, who's not living with an abuser, for her phone number.

Time to Break Free

Day 68

There is a difference between privacy and keeping secrets. Fifty-seven percent of the women battered by their male partners never discuss their abuse with anyone.[1] My secrets keep me from my personal healing and will continue to haunt me. It's important for me to know where I can share my secrets and feel safe. I don't have to share them with abusers or their friends. I can share in a support group or with a therapist and know these people will respect my privacy. I respect my own privacy by not telling people outside my support group about my past, especially when I first meet them. New relationships are just that— new. I can develop new memories and new experiences by not letting the past interfere. Healthy boundaries include giving the trust in new relationships time to grow by not sharing too much, too soon.

1. The Commonwealth Fund, *First Comprehensive National Health Survey of American Women Finds Them at Significant Risk,* news release (New York: The Commonwealth Fund, July 14, 1993).

Day 69

As hard as it may seem, as upset or alone as I may feel, as overwhelmed and confused as I may be, I promise myself not to abuse alcohol or other drugs during this time of healing. Substance abuse won't solve anything or help anyone. Besides, the feelings that I would be trying to get rid of would still be there when the bottle is empty. I can survive this healing process. Even if I don't believe it, I will act as if I believe it and keep telling myself I believe it. I promise myself to get through this healing process clean and sober. If I feel that I need to attend a Twelve Step meeting, I'll go to one. Some Twelve Step meetings are open to women only. I can call Twelve Step groups (their numbers are listed through information) and ask for a schedule of meetings. If I don't think I have a drug or alcohol problem, I will still promise myself a healing process without alcohol or drugs.

Time to Break Free

Day 70

Domestic violence and abuse are progressive. Abusers always want more and more control; therefore, their behavior becomes more aggressive or abusive in order to achieve this. If a relationship is verbally abusive, there's a good chance that someday it will become physically abusive. If a relationship is already physically abusive, there's a good chance the abuse will occur more often and become more violent. Now that I know about the progressive nature of abuse, my belief that "it might be different next time" takes on a whole new meaning. If my abuser has hit me already, the next time he hits me could be worse or even fatal. No battered woman ever said, "My abuser pushed me for twenty years." Today I will look at domestic violence differently. It doesn't get better, it gets worse, and I won't let it happen to me.

Day 71

Sometimes I feel like I'm competing with other abused women. I may hear or take part in conversations in which women are comparing situations or abusers: "If you think that's bad, listen to this" or, "Your husband may have pushed you around, but mine treated me much worse!" This competition doesn't help anyone. We simply want others to know how much we've been hurt; we want to be heard, and we want compassion. There is a way to feel heard without comparing myself to others. Expressing my feelings about the abuse instead of the details of what happened helps me move forward in my healing process. "When he pushed me, I felt afraid, angry, and alone" is a healing statement. When I learn to speak in this manner, I find that all abused women have shared the same types of feelings. This helps me better understand other people as well as myself.

Sometimes I feel sad or depressed and think I'm doing something wrong. With all the work I'm doing to change my life, shouldn't I feel happy all the time? No. Sadness is just as much a part of life as happiness. Just as all the seasons are part of nature, all my feelings are part of me. Would I awaken on a rainy day and refuse to let it rain? Would I claim that I'm going to do everything I can to stop the rain? No. When it rains, it rains. I accept the fact that there are times when I feel sad. I will let it be a part of being human.

Day 73

Today I will practice saying no. There have been many times in my life when I wanted to say it but was afraid. Even now, I may still be afraid. But I will say it anyway, if no is what I really mean. When someone asks me a question or offers a suggestion, I will stop and think about what I want before I respond. I will practice saying no to myself first. Do I really want to do the favor being asked of me? Is it okay with me that friends come to dinner? Is it good for me to attend a party or event? When I learn to say no to myself in simple matters, it becomes easier to say no to others. There have been times I went along with others to avoid conflict, or because I didn't know what I wanted. Today I will listen to myself and express myself. I have the right to say no.

It is okay to be compassionate and care about other people. But it's not okay to give up my needs to take care of someone else. When I do this, I am being "codependent." Today I will learn about this word. I will buy a book about codependency, go to the library and read about it, or attend a support group for women who have this problem. Codependency made it difficult to leave my abuser. Today I promise myself to learn all I can about codependency, but I also realize I don't have to learn it in one day. If this new information feels overwhelming, I can talk about it in my support group or with my therapist.

Day 75

Today I will practice detachment by letting go of things I can't control. Detachment means standing back and looking at a situation without having a hand in it. Watching fireworks is practicing detachment. Flying a kite is not. Allowing friends the freedom to have their own opinions is practicing detachment. Feeling compelled to change their minds is not. Watching a child create her own drawing is practicing detachment. Holding her hand while she draws is not. I can't control other people, their actions, or their beliefs by forcing them to act or believe as I do. Detachment helps me see the big picture, since I can see things more clearly from a distance. Today, and from now on, I will practice taking care of myself by detaching from people or situations that aren't good for me. Today I will pay close attention to when I am trying to force the issue, and I'll remember that my time would be better spent leaving it alone.

Time to Break Free

Day 76

Anger is very common in women who have been abused, especially once they stop blaming themselves and realize what they have endured. If I feel angry, I will allow myself that anger. During my abuse, many feelings stopped working, leaving me numb. Now that I'm recovering from the pain, my feelings are beginning to come back. For no apparent reason, I may feel angry or even start crying over little things. Even though my feelings may be painful or confusing, I am glad they're returning.

Day 77

Once I have learned to set my boundaries, others may try to ignore them or accuse me of being selfish. I know my boundaries have been crossed when I begin to feel uncomfortable inside, and I need to pay attention to this feeling. If others are used to relating to me in a certain way, and I'm changing, it usually means they have to change too. They may resist this change, but I'm not here to make other people happy; I'm here to make myself happy. If I don't want to change my mind about a boundary I've set, I don't have to. Other people will have to learn to live with the "new me." I recognize this new attitude as a sign that I'm getting stronger every day.

Time to Break Free

Day 78

New feelings may seem uncomfortable at first. I may be used to feeling afraid and anxious, or depressed and alone. In my new life, I may begin to feel joy or happiness, or peace and calm. These new feelings are signs that I'm changing and learning how to accept my new way of thinking. Feeling peaceful means I'm healing from all the crises in my past. If I confuse feeling peaceful with feeling bored, I need to remind myself that the absence of fear or crisis takes awhile to get used to. I am glad to welcome my new feelings and emotions; they are one way to know how well I'm doing.

Day 79

Today I will stop trying to do for others that which they can do for themselves, or that which they are not willing to do for themselves. I can't change other people or control how they feel and what they do. I can only be responsible for me. I don't buy self-help books for other people, hoping they'll read them and change. I don't write lists for other people, hoping they can improve their lives. I don't clip magazine or newspaper articles, hoping to help someone else with their problems. Becoming overly involved with helping others is one way I avoid helping myself or looking at my own problems. For now, I will detach from the problems of others and focus on myself and what I need to do.

In my new life, I sometimes feel a lack of excitement. I might miss the old adrenaline rush I used to get during a crisis. Even though I didn't like being in a crisis, the feeling I had in my body became familiar to me. I can find new activities or interests that feel exhilarating but that aren't harmful to me or others. It could be the excitement of enjoying a carnival ride, winning a race, playing a party game with friends, learning a new hobby or craft, or watching a suspenseful movie. These are just some things I might do to give my life some excitement without creating a crisis. When I feel like something is missing, I will try to pinpoint what it is and think about filling the emptiness with something that's good for me.

Day 81

As I begin to understand the dynamics of domestic violence, I might want to reach out and help others who have been abused. I might want to share all I've learned and tell them things I think they need to know. I must remember where I came from and how I felt before, or right after, I left my abuser. Even though I'm not an expert and might not feel comfortable giving advice, there are five statements I can use that might help someone who thinks they can't leave an abuser.

1) I'm afraid for your safety.
2) I'm afraid for the safety of your children.
3) It's only going to get worse.
4) You don't deserve to be treated that way.
5) I have a phone number to give you when you're ready to talk with someone about this problem. (Have a hot-line number ready.)

Any one of these statements helps me stay detached. Even if I decide to go ahead and share all I've learned, I must realize that others need to be ready, just like I needed to be.

Time to Break Free

Day 82

There are times when I imagine having a new relationship. It's very important for me to realize that, unless I learn all I can about abusive relationships, it's likely I will end up in another one. When certain types of relationships become familiar, people are drawn to certain types of people. A person may appear to be different or better than my previous relationship choices, but if I don't learn all I can about changing the type of person I'm attracted to, I will most likely choose another abuser. Today I promise to learn more about relationship patterns and about recognizing abusive people before I get into new relationships. With all the pain I've been through and all the work I'm doing, the last thing I want in my life is another abuser. I will learn all I can to make sure it doesn't happen again.

Day 83

I will go through a phase in my life where talking about my abuse helps me. It's a healing process that's necessary, as long as I talk to the right people. Once I have faced the past, talked about it, and begun to heal, I will slowly let go of my need to relive the crisis. Then I will no longer need to talk about the abuse over and over again. I can reveal my secrets, work on each problem, and move on. The time it takes to heal is different for everyone, and I can trust that eventually I will know the difference between facing the pain in order to heal, and just reliving the past.

Time to Break Free

Day 84

I am becoming aware of when I am being needy. It's healthy to need others, and even healthier to ask for help. There are many agencies and people willing to help me, but I have to do my part as well. When I let others do for me what I can do for myself, I remain a prisoner in my own life. It may feel easier to allow others to do the footwork for me, or to manipulate others into giving me what I want, but true freedom comes from taking responsibility for myself. I am willing to accept help, and when I've learned how, I help myself.

Day 85

Sometimes, after being on my own for a while, I might forget the bad things that have happened to me and start to miss my abuser. I may think the past was partly my fault and wonder if things could change in the future. I wonder if I should call, just to say hello. On these days, I will make a list of all the ways my abuser hurt me, and how I felt when that happened. I will put the list in a place I see often, like on the refrigerator door or the bathroom mirror. Whenever I start missing my abuser, I will read my abuse list.

It is common for children from domestically violent environments to take on characteristics of either the victim or the abuser. They may be withdrawn, be fearful, or act as if everyone is out to get them. They may also become verbally abusive, critical, disobedient, angry, or violent. While this is normal, it is not acceptable. Children act out in these ways because of things they've seen or heard in the past, and they are in need of help. Today I can help my children by being aware of their behavior and, most of all, by listening to their feelings about what has happened. If they don't talk about their feelings, I ask them. When they open up to me, I do not judge or criticize them. I have been through a lot, and so have they. If I am wondering whether my children need professional help, I will get a professional opinion. While I'm their mother and I love them, I realize I might not have all the answers.

Day 87

After all this time, things might still remind me of my abuser. A song, an event, a movie, a holiday, or anything else we once shared may stir feelings inside me that I haven't felt for quite a while. I'm aware that these feelings don't necessarily mean I'm "backsliding." I'm simply having feelings. I might not even know where they came from or why I'm having them. I allow myself to feel these feelings and let them go. I can be thankful for the ability to feel again. I can continue to tell myself that I've moved on, I'm in a different place now, and I can let the past be the past.

Time to Break Free

Day 88

Poor decisions I made in the past might still make others distrust my ability to make wise choices. I admit that, in the past, my perception was clouded, and I had trouble doing what was best for me and my children. In times when I "zoned out," I couldn't see what was happening to me, and I lacked the awareness of real danger. At that time I wasn't able to ask for or get what I needed. But now I'm learning how to make healthy and wise decisions, taking care of myself and my children. Other people may want me to prove myself to them, but the only person I have to prove anything to is myself. I am a thoughtful, responsible, strong, confident, and courageous woman.

Day 89

Even now, old feelings or thoughts may sneak into my new way of thinking. I may wonder if things could be different between my abuser and myself, if he really could change, and if our lives could be the way I have always wanted them to be. When this happens, I can determine how much I've learned and grown by how long I entertain these thoughts. In the beginning they may have lasted hours, days, or even weeks. Now they may only last a few seconds or minutes. When I have these thoughts, I realize I'm only wishing things could be different, and almost immediately I come back to the reality of today. I'm not angry with myself for hoping; I am proud that I can let go of false hopes so quickly.

Time to Break Free

Day 90

Today's society holds different beliefs about abused women. Many people judge us with statements like, "If it was so bad, why didn't she leave?" or, "She must have liked getting hit, or she wouldn't have stayed." These comments come from people who are ignorant about the issues confronted by battered women. In the past, fearing I would be judged, I may have felt too ashamed to admit being abused. Being ashamed may have stopped me from leaving sooner, or prevented me from seeking help earlier in the relationship. I may have made excuses for my abuser or lied about how I had been hurt. I know now that feeling ashamed did not help me and that I had no reason to be ashamed. The abuse done to me wasn't my fault. Today, whether or not I tell others about my past, I am filled with pride that I am now an ex-battered woman.

Day 91

Sometimes I get confused about other people's behavior. In the past, someone else's jealousy may have felt like love to me. When other people made decisions for me, I felt they cared about me and were "taking care" of me. Love and care do not mean obsessing over other people's behavior or trying to control them. Love and care mean allowing others the right to live their own lives. I need not be taken care of because I'm an adult, not a child. Today I will take responsibility, even when I'm afraid, for taking care of myself.

Time to Break Free

Day 92

It's common among abused children, or children who have witnessed abuse, to have distorted memories. They may confuse some incidents with others, and the details may run together. They may forget what really happened, when it happened, or what was said. While memories of details may be exaggerated or confused, memories of their feelings are usually quite accurate. I can detach from my own feelings and listen to the feelings of my children. When they discuss past events, not remembering exact details, I don't need to correct them. I may also suffer from memory lapses and be unable to remember exactly what happened during certain incidents, but I, too, have a clear picture of the feelings I had at the time. Our memories may not be precise, but our experiences were very real. My job is not to correct the memories; it is to understand the feelings behind them.

Day 93

Today I will look at my beliefs about sex. Have I given in to sex, or was I forced to have sex when I didn't want it? Have I used sex as a way to feel loved? Have I used sex to get something I wanted? Today I will take a look at my past sexual behavior, how it has benefited me, and how it has hurt me. I won't feel overcome with guilt or shame. I understand that I did the best I could and that the past is in the past. Starting today, my attitude toward sex can be different.

Time to Break Free

Day 94

Today I can write a letter to my abuser, knowing I'm not going to mail it. I can tell him everything: how I feel, how his behavior has affected my life, what his actions have done to the children, how I felt while he was abusing me, or how I felt about his broken promises. I can be angry and write huge words that take up the entire page. I can swear at him, call him names, and say all I've wanted to say for so long. I can say anything because I'm not going to mail it. After I write the letter, I may choose to read it to someone with whom I feel safe. I can choose to put it away and read it again one year from now, or I can choose to burn it. Whatever I decide to do with it, I will write the letter.

Day 95

Now that I've learned more about my relationship patterns, I may feel frightened when I think
about entering a new relationship, fearing the
same thing might happen again. This is normal.
It's better for me to wait until I'm comfortable
being on my own before I consider dating. An
important part of my healing is becoming aware
of what I want in a future relationship. I can
make a list of traits I want in an "ideal relationship," and I can list everything I want in a partner.
I will keep my list in a safe place and read it often.
Even though I may not be ready for a relationship
now, it's important to be aware of what I want in
the future.

Whenever I meet someone new, male or female, I remember my "ideal relationship" list. My list for a partner also represents most of the things I would like in my friendships. When I'm deciding whether I want someone to be my friend, I think of the things on my list that are most important to me, and where I'm willing to compromise. "Respects my boundaries" should be at the top of my list for any relationship, and when I meet someone new, I pay attention to the signals that show me if they have this quality. I may set boundaries as simple as, "Please don't call after eight o'clock" or, "I can't see you tomorrow because I have other plans" or, "I don't feel comfortable inviting you over yet." If these simple boundaries are ignored, I will let the relationship go, knowing that once someone ignores simple boundaries, they will most likely ignore the more important ones. Better to get out now than to repeat past mistakes.

Day 97

Men aren't always the abusers. Women can be controlling, overbearing, and abusive as well. I don't want anyone in my life who tries to control me or prevents me from making my own decisions. Warning signs can tell me when a relationship might be harmful for me. Does she belittle others, even when joking? Does he tell me how to dress? Does she offer opinions or advice on decisions I should make, what I should do, or how I should raise my children? Does he want to move too fast in the relationship or friendship? Did she have an abusive childhood? Does he want to "take care" of me or "protect" me? Does she want to control my social life or the friends I have? These are only a few signals that tell me when a relationship is headed for disaster. It takes a long time to really get to know someone, and I promise myself to take each relationship slowly. I will tune in to the warning signs and end any relationship if I'm too uncomfortable to continue it. I have the right to have relationships in my life that are good for me and my children.

Time to Break Free

Day 98

It has been a long time since I've been with my abuser. I feel stronger and stronger each day. With newly found strength comes the courage to work a little more on myself. The more I work, the greater the chances are that I will not end up in a relationship with an abuser again. Today I will make a list of the ways I have grown and the things I have learned in the past ninety-eight days. The best thing about breaking free is that I now make my own choices.

Day 99

Even though I wasn't abusive, I still played a part in the abusive relationship. Whenever my abuser began abusive behavior, I usually reacted in the same way, whatever that was. In domestic violence, the abuser and the victim have roles that they play, again and again. Today I realize and accept that I played a part in the abuse. Whether I was outspoken or timid, I played a part. By realizing this, I can begin to respond differently in conversations with abusive people, whether they are from my past or someone new. Today I will choose not to play the same role anymore. Even though I can't change someone else, I will take responsibility for myself by changing how I react.

Time to Break Free

Day 100

Today I've been free for one hundred days. In the time it took me to use this book, approximately 960,000 beatings against women occurred in the United States.[2] This time I wasn't one of them. I've come so far, and I feel stronger and more confident than I've ever felt in my life. There are a lot of people who helped me when I couldn't help myself, who believed in me when I didn't believe in myself, who encouraged me to succeed when I felt like a failure. I'm here to say:

> thanks to my spiritual beliefs,
> whatever they may be,
> to all of you, and to me,
> I have my life back.

2.   The Commonwealth Fund, *First Comprehensive National Health Survey of American Women Finds Them at Significant Risk,* news release (New York: The Commonwealth Fund, July 14, 1993).

Suggested Reading

Beattie, Melody. *Beyond Codependency: And Getting Better All the Time.* Center City, Minn.: Hazelden, 1989.

——.*Codependent No More: How to Stop Controlling Others and Start Caring for Yourself.* 2d ed. Center City, Minn.: Hazelden, 1992.

——.*The Language of Letting Go.* Center City, Minn.: Hazelden, 1990.

Engel, Beverly. *Encouragements for the Emotionally Abused Woman: Wisdom and Hope for Women at Any Stage of Emotional Abuse Recovery.* New York: Fawcett Columbine, 1993.

NiCarthy, Ginny. *Getting Free: You Can End Abuse and Take Back Your Life.* Seattle: Seal Press, 1997.

NiCarthy, Ginny, and Sue Davidson. *You Can Be Free: An Easy-to-Read Handbook for Abused Women.* Seattle: Seal Press, 1997.

Renzetti, Claire. *Violent Betrayal: Partner Abuse in Lesbian Relationships.* Newbury Park, Calif.: Sage Publications, 1992.

Statman, Jan Berliner. *The Battered Woman's Survival Guide: Breaking the Cycle.* Dallas: Taylor Publishing, 1995.

White, Evelyn C. *Chain Chain Change: For Black Women in Abusive Relationships.* Seattle: Seal Press, 1994.

Zambrano, Myra M. *Mejor Sola Que Mal Acompanada: Para la Mujer Golpeada* (For the Latina in an abusive relationship). Seattle: Seal Press, 1985.

Resources

Battered Women's Justice Project
4032 Chicago Avenue South
Minneapolis, MN 55407
(800) 903-0111

National Council on Child Abuse and Family
    Violence
1155 Connecticut Avenue Northwest, Suite 400
Washington, DC 20036
(800) 222-2000
(202) 429-6695

National Domestic Violence Hotline
(800) 799-SAFE (7223)
TDD (800) 787-3224

National Victim Center
2111 Wilson Boulevard, Suite 300
Arlington, VA 22201
(800) FYI-CALL (394-2255)
Provides information and referrals, not crisis
    counseling.

WOMAN, Inc.
333 Valencia Street, Suite 251
San Francisco, CA 94103
(415) 864-4722
For lesbians in violent relationships.

Women of Color Task Force Against Domestic
  Violence
P. O. Box 1743
Aurora, CO 80040
(303) 696-9196

About the Author

From the age of sixteen, Judith Smith experienced one abusive relationship after another and, at the age of thirty-nine, found herself in the most violent and terrifying relationship of her life. She endured the abuse and emotional turmoil for three years before deciding to break free.

Once Smith emerged from the insanity of that relationship, she realized that she wanted to change her life. She wanted to understand why she had felt so emotionally chained to her abuser, and why she had never been able to enjoy a loving and fulfilling relationship. She joined a support group that offered education for battered women and attended every week, oftentimes more, for over nine months. She went to counseling and obtained counseling for her children with an agency specializing in domestic violence and abuse. She then attended a training program to become a domestic violence counselor.

It is from her personal experience as a battered woman that Smith understands how emotionally overwhelmed and vulnerable people feel in the beginning stages of leaving an abusive relationship. *Time to Break Free* is designed to be short, simple, and easy to understand. It is written for the first one hundred days after a person leaves an abuser. This is a most difficult time, as many people, unaware of their options or lacking education on the subject of abuse, return to their abusers or find similar relationships.

One of the most common statements among newly aware abused women is, "I just didn't know." It is with this in mind, and with love, compassion, and hope, that Smith has written this book for women who are ready to take back their lives and begin the process of breaking free.

Smith currently resides in Roseville, California, and is the single mother of two young children. She has extensive experience as an educator, artist, publisher, graphic designer, and creative advertising specialist.

Hazelden Information and Educational Services is a division of the Hazelden Foundation, a not-for-profit organization. Since 1949, Hazelden has been a leader in promoting the dignity and treatment of people afflicted with the disease of chemical dependency.

The mission of the foundation is to improve the quality of life for individuals, families, and communities by providing a national continuum of information, education, and recovery services that are widely accessible; to advance the field through research and training; and to improve our quality and effectiveness through continuous improvement and innovation.

Stemming from that, the mission of this division is to provide quality information and support to people wherever they may be in their personal journey—from education and early intervention, through treatment and recovery, to personal and spiritual growth.

Although our treatment programs do not necessarily use everything Hazelden publishes, our bibliotherapeutic materials support our mission and the Twelve Step philosophy upon which it is based. We encourage your comments and feedback.

The headquarters of the Hazelden Foundation

is in Center City, Minnesota. Additional treatment facilities are located in Chicago, Illinois; New York, New York; Plymouth, Minnesota; St. Paul, Minnesota; and West Palm Beach, Florida. At these sites, we provide a continuum of care for men and women of all ages. Our Plymouth facility is designed specifically for youth and families.

For more information on Hazelden, please call **1-800-257-7800**. Or you may access our World Wide Web site on the Internet at **www.hazelden.org**.